MERAKI

THE ESSENCE OF SOUL

SHINY BENJAMIN

Made with ♥ on the Notion Press Platform
www.notionpress.com

Dedicated

To my near and dear ones who believed in me
for them I repay my regards as blessing.

Contents

Contents

Foreword

The poetry from the pen of Shiny Benjamin deals with variety of themes ranging from romantic to deep philosophic subject seems to have a deep penetration into mystery of human life. If we want to enjoy the taste of honeyed diction and natural fall of rhythms, we must read her book for literary ecstasy.

-by Mohd Gulrej Khan

Preface

This book of poem is inspired from the human feelings and the surroundings, that triggered me to pen down. Moreover it is a connection of my thoughts dealing with myriad encounters of realistic events in life. The aim of writing this book is to share my thoughts and feelings with others.

Acknowledgements

"Gratitude is something which we can never owe".

But still in the list of being grateful I can never forget to thank all those people who have travelled with me in my life journey and supported me in my writing without ifs and buts. I would deeply acknowledge my debt to my late uncle Sushil Redford Benjamin who has always been my mentor.

My heartfelt thanks to my husband Mr Abhinav Shukla, mom Mrs Grace Lorna Benjamin, dad Mr Shelfey Carey Benjamin, younger sister Anna Benjamin Datta , mother in law Manorama Shukla and father in law Mr John Subodh Shukla . I also owe thanks to all my close friends who showed an unwavering trust and faith me.

My work would never be possible without the constant support and the vision of Notion Press team, the Publishing Manager ,the editor, the Cover designer and others who have supported me whole heartedly in my book.

Thanking you all

Prologue

"A powerful writing is more effective than thousand words as it creates an unforgettable history and unbelievable future."

This book is about the different genres, giving you a vast knowledge about various emotions of human. It has a uniqueness in the style of writing and touches every heart and soul. This book present the strong emotions of an author and that create a strong bond between the reader and author.

About The Author

Shiny Benjamin, the Author of "Meraki" is a teacher by profession. She has a charismatic personality which radiates the beauty of her thoughts.

Shiny's hardworking and dedicated nature makes her a tremendous writer. She has seen herself growing from seed to tree and had started writing when she was pursuing her Bachelors. She has a vision to become a great writer thus she has worked hard to achieve her dream.

Shiny wants leave a deep mark on mind and heart of the people through her writing and want to be an inspiration for others. Her writing always speak more of her feelings with whom anyone can connect. She wish to be a landmark in the field of writing.

She further says that if we want to achieve something in life hard work is important. Shortcut will never lead you to your success. She mentioned that "The joy of victory come to those who have see darkest nights" .

She is a Muse who stimulates others with her teaching and her writing.

Her most cherished quote is :-

"Outer beauty fades

Inner beauty radiates"

Which often inspired her to trust her inner strength. Having pure heart and soul is the priceless thing which a person can own in this materialistic life.

Her writing has a charm to elicit the attention of her readers. And also leaves a deep impact on their

mind and heart.
Her solo book "Hymn of heart " is a beautiful collection of poems and all her poems are beautifully crafted, they have a taste of freshness in it.

Her poems have been published in numerous anthologies. Here are the names of her few books in which she has contributed.
Which are as follows:-
1) Is it lockdown ya humari zindagi hai locked down
2) A walk down the lane
3) Daffodils
4) love Me Tomorrow
5) Wild Knows your name
6) Quilling Thoughts
7) Eccentric Humans
8) Power of Tradition
9) Scrivere Bellissimo
10) Garden of reminiscence
11) Did I make something wrong?
12) Mysterious Moments
13) Dreamy World
14) Life moves on

You can mail her on the Id given below
shinyjbenjamin@gmail.com

You can also follow her on Instagram
Shinyjbenjamin

With Love,
Shiny Benjamin

1. I have nothing to lose

Unless I am an open letter
you are able read me.
Let me be hidden, hiding
myself in those fold
I have nothing to lose.

Each folds depict my story
each verse is a nugatory.

Having lost myself what else
I wish to lose. I could not recognise
myself in a mirror, what do I call
myself as a deceiver or an imposter.

Hiding me inside my folds, unable
to breath,
None understood my situation as I
am suffocating,
I have lost my happiness but still wears
a smile, just to show the world how
strong am I.
I broke as no one dares to see
what going inside me or how deep

my pain is.
I have lost my placidity but still acting
with tranquillity.
I have nothing to lose.

2. Unfiltered Self

In the world of show off and masking ourselves to become a new entity. Somewhere we have forgotten to live our lives fairly.

For each new day we have different filters, for every situation we are putting new filter in our lives.

And have started losing our identity, our real self and our true version.

We have hidden ourselves underneath the filters and started living our lives accordingly.

Crude self is a nourishment for our healthy life, which make our relation strong, and has a power to change the strongest filter of faux into unfiltered self.

In the life of faux and filters we have grown so prominent that our real self has faded and to cover ourselves we have used filters, even to make ourselves more eminent we change according to the situation as we change our clothes.
At last we face identity crises which bring a great havoc in self identification.

3. Relations need no tags

We look out for those relations where we can sojourn for the whole life.

It is like the combination of coffee and cake enjoying each other's company. We feel sombre when one is empty.

It has its own taste laden with the quality of sweet and sour.

We all put tags with each relations to specify the weightage in the bond. We don't need any tags, no specifications just a bond where one can find a sojourn of togetherness.

Nothing is left in the name or brand, what will be left with us is a smidgen of love and belongingness, which is needed in bits and pieces of our life.

People look out for named relations. Sometimes relations without the name can heal much faster.

What is in a name!

where one can find a home in person.

4. Smelling like Summer

Chanting winds, dancing leaves
she found sojourn in her memories
she saw outside the broken window
zephyr passing by entered her room

And found smelling of memories like summer.
Serene smile, twinkling eyes she was
indulge in her reverie calling it as
memory.

Her tress falling on her face
rewinding the memory of her old days. she went on streets like smelling summer as a retreat.
On the clammy road, she walked alone listening to heart, feeling the blow of air remembering those summer days where she walked hand in hand. And singing those jingles of summer.

The smell of her tress was tropical fruit which remind her the compliment given by him when he breeze pass through her hair and give the sense of summer.
For her smallest memories smelled like a summer.

5. Unknown depth of shallowness

"Words became verse leaving its impact on mind. Looking at the person's mien will never give you the inkling of how deep the person can feel".

Shallowness of mine was always deceptive,
And the depth in me was never predictive.

Like a written verse on a paper has no feel,
But then in person what you see is just unreal.

The book which can be read by many,
Has in store twist and turns plenty.

Smell of the ink on those pages were so dark,
They seeped into the depth of life to embark.

My beautiful smile was always a guile,
Never letting other know what's there inside.

Ebullient nature with unassailable attitude,
No one will ever come to know I live in solitude.

I was half knowledge book of arcane,
With unknown depth of amaranthine.

6. Some stolen peace became my relief

Earnestly wanted it but couldn't receive,
Like barren mother wanted to conceive.

I asked someone to give me on credit,
But no one was ready to share it.

I wanted just a piece of a peace,
Stolen from my friend, indeed.

Made my pillow for the peaceful sleep,
Since many years I yearn so deep.

My mind was in the state of turmoil,
It gave me a momentary smile.

7. Bewitching Meadows

In the beautiful surroundings I want to flow,
In a search of peace on my toe.
Watching the colourful rainbow,
I feel, I could absorb and could glow.

Zephyr kissed my mien touching the cold
Leaves of willow,
Gently rubbing my cheeks, making it look mellow

Dancing flowers near my window,
Sang joyful song of all heights and shallows.

Hearing the distant melody of banjo
I stopped to enjoy in the nature's wallow

My mind is now gleaming like wild indigo,
I am stimulated by these bewitching meadows

8. Expectation never heals

"Patience makes a person better
But waiting makes them bitter "

Expectation steals the essence of any relation,
Making it decathect from the one we believed.
Trusted in years, to become a catalyst
for the salvation,
With the waning love, distance thrived.

Understanding is deprived of compassion,
Compatibility rejects the innocence .
Brackish feeling makes the bond ashen,
Spirit of togetherness was at ignorance.

Counting on each other will keep breathing,
But waiting will always lead to decline.
Expectation hurts but hope helps in believing,
To keep going in any relation, trust is amaranthine.

9. Stitching Bits and Pieces of Trust

This afternoon I was sitting
in my armchair with the bits
and pieces of my trust which
was lying on floor.

Poor me! Couldn't control my
tears, with those teary eyes I
tried to make out my sewing skills
I took my needle of hope and slide
the thread of love. Though being callow
in stitching I started my sewing.

Took bits and pieces of trust which
was lying on the floor. Trying to tuck
each pieces.

However to tuck each pieces was
so hard because these pieces were
the betrayal of those whom I ever loved.

Tucking each piece made me bleed
as their betrayal hits my fingers terribly.

My cloth of trust with needle of hope
and the thread of love couldn't amalgamate
the cloth of trust.

Ever since I left stitching my cloth of trust it
was left hanging forever to be stitch again

10. Be unique, Be you

In the summer sky
I was the wave of zephyr
People searching for the synonyms
I always looked for the antonyms
Moving in the bulk is not an option
Making the own way was my determination

Like zephyr, I swayed as I wam the master
of my own
Never walking on the trail left by them
When people thought I am done, I came back with a bang.

Being you , and being different is not a fault
Your uniqueness will give the people a great jolt
In the sky I am the rainbow which has
a unique quality and has a rare beauty.

I violate the rule to make my own
When people thought that I am unable
but I am never weary of making it able.
Let the foot of mine accompany with
the rhythm of waves of those zephyr
who pave its own destiny.

11. Folds of human nature

From changing of seasons to changing of life humans have changed too. As a detached leaf looses its identity and become senseless likewise people too are deserted in their feelings and emotions and their senses becomes barren.

It is a human quality to get attached and then detached after losing the interest in them . The mind set of them are to use like tissue and throw it after the need is over.

This turn of mind tags every relation leaving bad taste in our mouth and then it makes difficult for a person to take up next relation as once bitten twice shy will always remember the bad taste left by them.

If we are stepping in someone's life, enter with a promise never to desert them at any cost.

Human have folds in their nature as you keep on unfolding it you will find a new face with unknown qualities. And it will become more difficult to realise which fold is true. Sometimes people are more harmful than the high risk product We can be cured by affect of risky product but it's impossible to recover from the humans sting.

12. Painting her brokenness

Colours bright, a new day a new life
fading night into the sky.
Raining happiness , painting her
brokenness.

Seasons lost touch yet bravely facing
the new era. Bare emotions got detached,
no words to say, no relation slayed.

Quietly she advanced, don't want to be a scape goat again.
Painting her brokenness
with the sanity.
Armouring herself with placidity.

No haste, no trauma she had played
with full drama. Her each cracks were
shining with different hues of rainbow beautifying her self
spirit.

Raising a toast to herself for the audacity of painting her parameters where no one can trespass her periphery.

Her each cracks were marked with different hues and tags.
And those tags revealed how dauntless she is.
Painting her brokenness, she felt so free.

13. Attached with no string

Those mild showers fell on my skin,
tickling me, making me giggle, I never
felt so beautiful.

Your descent in my life has brought
the showers of love and made me
feel over the moon.

Our regale conversations were like
the smell of petrichor, inducing me
in hygge.

Those zephyr touched my cheeks and
tress with its soft glide , I felt that it is
your touch which made my feelings
dance.

Season became different for me. Autumn
felt as spring, summer felt like rainy and
winter were not too cozy but I was tickled
pink in his thought.

This beauty of togetherness became the epitome of our love where we are attached to each other with our souls.

14. Moving on is bitter but much better

Like a sailing boat you have sail
across the sea even if there is a
lot of horrendous waves coming
in your way.

Sometimes in our life many situation
will arise where you have to move
on instead to cling at the same place.

The day you will realise that dwelling
to the same place will lead you
nowhere.

That moment will set you out
in that sailing boat where you have
to stride forward rather than becoming
the victim of your past or letting you
drown in the memories of those days
where once you find solace.
"Moving on is bitter but much better".

15. Flight of Faith

Umpteen attempts were failed,
Positivity peep to refrain.
Reviving spirits got passive,
Hope in nerves thrashes.
Underlying vigour ebb and flow,
Mustering courage was never my foe.
Insurgence surpasses, faith rose,
Deeply enacted to my soul.
Singing my efforts of fight,
Levitating my fearless faith.
Soaring to the unknown sky,
Never underestimating my flight.

16. On a Route To Life

Life has distinct pages,
Tossing and turning through
each phases,
Arcane and undeniable.

Holding many offers,
Getting many denials,
We are a boat which sails
through every trials.

Someday success kisses our
true worth,
But sometimes failures dances
to tempt us,
Choose to Prioritise ourselves to
unleash the barrier.

17. A Ray of Esperance

Twilit was abound,
Like a dungeon it has surrounded.

Scepticism was stretching in and out,
Clutched my throat, making it parched
as a drought.

Like an unfavoured child yearning for smile,
Knocking every closed doors of life.

A ray of esperance ripped in with vigour,
Ebbing towards glimmer.

Blessedness took a flight,
To cease the treacherous night.

18. Togetherness - (Somonka)

Countless sighs I took
Each time I breathe, I relive
Your ebullient smile
is an aurora where the
rainbow sings on horizon

Heart twitterpated
Swaying to lose my senses
deliberately
Melting in the azure sky
to become colour of love

19. True beauty - (Haiku)

Let the beauty of
Your heart shine through your words,
as it reflects your soul.

Testimonials

Here are the testimonials from people who read my poems

Unknown Depth Of Shallowness

A beautiful way to describe the intrinsic value of the people's character, or lack of IT.

I love how you describe shallowness on people, shallow people are very easy to read, to predict and to deal with.

The more depth there is in a person, the tastier and complex the interactions the more experiences are present and offered.

Complexity in people is an amazing characteristic, multi-phases brings a wow factor where we never stop learning about an individual. This part is critical for expanding and learning from one another.

I love your work,

It resonates with my teachings on how only complex people can read other complex individuals.

You can't speak butterfly language with a caterpillar.

-by Joshua Van Joseph

Unfiltered Self

This is a beautiful and colorful reflection of how people are losing their identity, I love how you describe how day by day people's identity fades away and a sublime mask covers people's faces without knowing.

A profound thought that people need to put back into perspective. In the rush of trying to fit into a superficial world, we are losing ourselves.

-by Joshua Van Joseph

Folds Of Human Nature

This poem composed in philosophic tone unfolds the mystery of human nature. Its theme explores the cause of pain and melancholy and thus ends with a message how to prevent from bitter negative melancholic vibes. Quote fresh and brimming with emotion makes this poem worth reading.

-by Mohd Gulrej Khan

Some Stolen Peace Became My Relief

It is a poetic quest for peace and pleasure. The straightforward tone in which poetic lines are composed directly enters the bosom of the readers. Compact and precise poetic thought adds to the very charm of the poem.

-by Mohd Gulrej Khan

I'm Just Speechless

I'm so fortunate to read the poetry of Ms. S. Benjamin. They're so touching, her words have thrilled my mind, I'm so eloquent with her poetry and write up. I'm just speechless.

-Rechal Xavier

Thank You Note For The Readers

"A bond is a beautiful relationship between the two people"
I am immensely grateful to my readers for a beautiful bond created through this book. You all complete me as without you no books can be reviewed.

www.ingramcontent.com/pod-product-compliance
Lightning Source LLC
LaVergne TN
LVHW090130160826
845673LV00016B/1188

* 9 7 9 8 8 9 1 8 6 3 0 4 0 *